Lighthouses

All photographs by Philip Plisson, with the exception of:
page 10 copyright © Christophe Le Potier
photographs on pages 14, 19, 31, 42, 43, 48, 49, 61 copyright © Guillaume Plisson

Designed by Jay Colvin

Library of Congress Cataloging-in-Publication Data has been applied for
ISBN: 0-8109-5958-5

Copyright © 2005 Éditions De La Martinière Jeunesse, France
2, rue Christine – 75006 Paris
English translation copyright © 2005 Harry N. Abrams, Inc.

Printed and bound in Belgium
10 9 8 7 6 5 4 3 2 1

Harry N. Abrams, Inc.
100 Fifth Avenue
New York, NY 10011
www.abramsbooks.com

Abrams is a subsidiary of

Lighthouses

Photographs by
PHILIP PLISSON ⚓

Text by
Francis Dreyer

Drawings by
Daniel Dufour

HARRY N. ABRAMS, INC., PUBLISHERS

CONTENTS

The Lighthouse Collector

I collect lighthouses the way other people collect stamps, coins or key-rings.

I am an *amateur* of lighthouses, you might say, for that word comes from the French word for "love" and I love lighthouses. This love took hold of me pretty early, in fact as soon as I was old enough to go sailing with my family. I have to admit I was lucky, leaving from the harbor at La Trinité, for there were lots of navigation lights all around us. There were those that could be reached from land and those stuck on isolated rocks, which you could sail around in good weather. And then as night fell there was the Goulphar. It gave out two flashes every ten seconds. By day it was invisible, thirty miles away on the island of Belle-Île. But it is perched almost 300 feet above sea level, and by night its powerful flashes could be seen from our house. So you can imagine how excited I was one summer afternoon when I found myself at the foot of this 170-foot tower. My brothers and sister and I had moored at Le Palais and then bicycled over. The lighthouse was open to visitors and one of the three keepers was at the door. A little knot of expectant people was gathering under his eyes. We were given a short history and told that—of course—this was the most beautiful and the most powerful lighthouse in the world (or very nearly . . .) and equipped with the very latest technology. Keepers are always in love with their lighthouses and talk about them as if they were an old lady they were privileged to be looking after. One piece of advice: Save your breath for the stairs. At the Goulphar, there are

256 between you and the lantern! Out of breath and thrilled to the marrow, we were met at the top by a second keeper. And he had to answer all my questions, such as: "How do you make it flash so brilliantly? How do you make it flash twice every ten seconds?" This was the point at which the name Augustin Fresnel entered my memory forever. For he invented a set of lenses that could confine the light to a single beam and multiply its strength so its brilliance would carry beyond the horizon. Here before me were two superb Fresnel optics, as they are called. They were lovingly buffed and burnished. Every night they alerted sailors to their whereabouts. And every night they gave me a wink in far-off La Trinité. Since then I have learned that during the nineteenth century the French coastline was lined with lighthouses equipped with Fresnel lenses. And this piece of French technology was adopted all over the maritime world, so that every night thousands of lighthouses light up the sea with the aid of Mr. Fresnel. To date, I've visited some 500 lighthouses all over the globe. It may be more—I love them so much I have long since stopped counting—and I still feel the same excitement every time. For me, they are haunted by their function: saving the seaman from drowning.

Today there are no lynx-eyed keepers watching from the lantern or taking care of their "old lady lighthouse." They have been taken ashore because it is cheaper to use machines. But make no mistake: The sea goes on battering at the foundations of our lighthouse heritage, weakening them day by day. Does anybody care? I hope you will when you have read this book. And now— come on! Up to the lantern!

—Philip Plisson

Signs at Sea

At the mouth of the Trieux River on the Côtes d'Armor in France, the La Croix Lighthouse resembles a medieval castle. Two masonry beacons signal the approaches to the island of Bréhat.

Around the world there are all kinds of signs for ships to steer by. Whether out at sea or onshore, these signs are the "landmarks" of the sea. One of these is the lighthouse, which sends out very powerful beams of light. Ships sailing through the dark can see them from miles away. There are also short-range light signals, such as range lights (which guide ships through narrow channels) and harbor lights. Buoys are also used to guide ships; they float on the water and may have lights on them. Some signs, like foghorns, work by noise rather than light. The simplest signs are physical markers, such as beacons. The most sophisticated are radio or satellite beacons. There are hundreds of thousands of such devices around the coasts of the world. The job of looking after them falls to the Marine Aids to Navigation and Lighthouse Authorities. In the United States of America this is the Coast Guard. All year round thousands of people are working to ensure the safety of ships at sea—and thanks to them, today's sailors no longer live in fear of being shipwrecked.

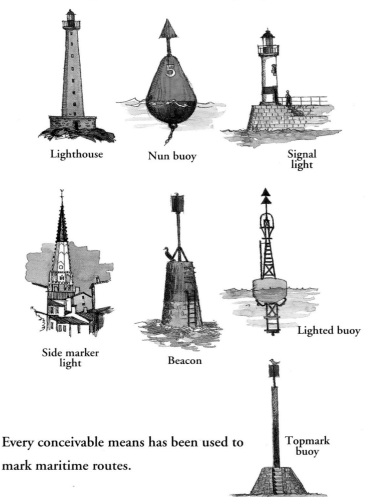

Lighthouse   Nun buoy   Signal light

Side marker light   Beacon   Lighted buoy

Topmark buoy

Every conceivable means has been used to mark maritime routes.

Lighthouses in Ancient Times

The Tower of Hercules in northern Spain is the oldest lighthouse still functioning. It is 225 feet high.

Lighthouses have not always been there to guide ships. In the distant past, ships sailed very close to shore and tried not to lose sight of it—which meant they traveled only by day. When night fell, the sailors would ground the ship on a beach to protect it from storms, and set off again in the morning. There were no light signals because there was no need for them. But as countries began to trade with each other, the traffic on the seas increased. Some harbors installed lights, though they were not very powerful. Then came the construction of lighthouses. For a harbor, lighthouses were like neon lights in a shop window, attracting ships and commerce. The most famous one was at Alexandria in Egypt, where the Nile flows into the Mediterranean Sea. Built around 300 BCE, it was made of white marble and took its name from the island where it stood: Pharos. The oldest lighthouse still in use today is the Tower of Hercules, built by the Romans on the Spanish coast near La Coruña in the second century CE. At night its light can be seen from up to thirty-two nautical miles out to sea. And if you want to see the optic (the big lamp unit in a lighthouse) you have to go up 242 steps. That's a lot of steps!

Recent discoveries in Egypt have allowed archeologists to reconstruct the appearance of the Alexandrian lighthouse, which dates from 300 BCE.

How Did the Early Lighthouses Work?

John Doherty, keeper of the Tory Island Lighthouse in Ireland, fits a new bulb into the Fresnel optic.

Lighthouses have not always been powered by electricity. Until the middle of the eighteenth century they featured enormous metal-grid baskets in which wood or charcoal was burned to create a signal fire. The metal basket that held the fire was situated on a broad platform at the top of the tower, and the flames were fanned by the wind. People had to carry fuel up the narrow spiral stairs on their backs. This was hard work: Every night lighthouse keepers had to take some 650 pounds of wood and charcoal up to the top of the tower. This was not their only job. They also had to stir the embers to make sure the light stayed bright. And in bad weather, the fire often had to be relit after it was put out by storms or rain. Something to shelter the fire was clearly needed—eventually glass walls were used to surround the flame and a copper dome was placed on top of these walls. Coal was deemed too dirty to be practical and the coal fires were replaced by oil-burning lamps. Then came electricity, and in the twentieth century, light bulbs as big as footballs were installed. The bulbs used today are no larger than the ones you use in your home. Now that's progress!

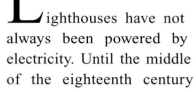

During the eighteenth century, lighthouse fires used all kinds of fuel: wood, charcoal, garbage, seaweed, and even fish oil.

Where Were Lighthouses Built?

▲ Ponza Island Lighthouse (Italy)

▼ Bird's Rock Lighthouse (Canada)

Lighthouses were built wherever there was danger to ships: rocky promontories, desert islands, ice, or turbulent seas.

▼ Ar-Men Lighthouse (France)

Lighthouses serve three purposes: They show a ship where the coastline is, help it know which direction to steer in, and alert it to dangers that may be invisible, like rocks below the surface of the sea. So lighthouses should be the first thing a ship sees when it approaches the coast, even before it enters a navigation channel leading to the port itself. This explains why lighthouses were built in very specific places, for example, on rocky headlands that jut out into the sea, on rocks that might tear open a ship's hull, and on hills where they can be lined up with other lights to mark a path to the harbor. They can therefore be divided into three types: coastal, island, and rock lighthouses. Beginning in the late eighteenth century, scientists mapped the seabed by using plummet lines (measuring lines with lead weights on them) to find places where rocks were near the surface. This information was used to decide where lighthouses were needed. Now sailors know what course they must steer to avoid invisible dangers; lighthouses send out their beams into the darkness to light sailors' paths.

Thousands of soundings had to be made for sea charts, which marked every rock and reef.

Coastal Lighthouses

▲ Slatteroy Lighthouse (Norway)　　　　　　　▼ Buchan Ness Lighthouse (Scotland)　　▲ Slyne Head Lighthouse (Ireland)　　　　　　▼ Cap Sim Lighthouse (Mor

Coastal lighthouses are surrounded by other buildings such as electricity-generating stations, farm buildings, shops, and cisterns. Six keepers looked after each lighthouse; including their families, that meant accommodation for some thirty people.

Coastal lighthouses are the most common kind of lighthouse. They line the coast, one every few miles, so that ships sailing toward land can find their way safely to harbor. Before electronic positioning systems, ships frequently steered in the wrong direction, especially when they were sailing far from land. Lighthouses warned ships that they were close to land and informed them which coast they were approaching. For this reason, coastal lighthouses are always very high buildings, often built on hills or cliff tops so that they can be seen from as far away as possible. They usually have living quarters for the keepers and their families, though these days lighthouses are almost all completely automatic. Some lighthouses stand right beside a port or at the mouth of a navigable river since these are important places for maritime traffic.

◀ St. John's Lighthouse (Ireland)

Island Lighthouses

On Skellig Michael Island in Ireland, the blustering wind continuously rakes the steep rock-cut path and it sometimes took several hours to bring equipment and fuel up to the lighthouse platform.

For a ship approaching the coast, islands are often the first indication of the mainland. So island lighthouses are to ships what runway approach lights are to planes. They must be visible from afar and their light has to be very intense. The Creac'h Lighthouse on the island of Ushant in Ouessant, France, was for a long time the most powerful in the world. It marked the very dangerous Ouessant shipway through which thousands of ships pass every year. Its beam could be seen from over fifty miles away. The inhabitants of the island sometimes thought that the sun had risen when the light went on! Some lighthouses, like the Rhinns of Islay in Scotland, were built on—or close to—large islands with their own villages and cultures. The lighthouse keepers' lives on Islay were quite enjoyable. But imagine the life of the keeper stuck on a tiny island at sea level or on top of terrifying cliffs like those of Skellig Michael in southwest Ireland! Conditions were harsh, the solitude was grim, and every time provisions came in, there was the long climb down to the harbor and back.

On small islands, it was difficult to provide for the family. Cows, chickens, rabbits, and a vegetable garden helped sustain daily life.

Rock Lighthouses

The first Longships Lighthouse was built 210 years ago. The current tower, below, built in 1875, is very narrow and was among the least comfortable in England.

Rocks sometimes reach the surface of the sea thousands of miles from the nearest coast. Such reefs can be invisible to ships and are very dangerous. They have to be marked by lighthouses that are built directly on top of them, hence the name "rock lighthouse." Until 1950, no signal light was permitted unless there was a lighthouse keeper to look after it. The keeper had to light and switch off the lantern, check the fuel level, and clean the lantern windows. These lighthouses also had living quarters. The keepers of rock lighthouses often led harsh lives. Their geographical isolation and the long months they spent away from their families intensified the loneliness they probably felt. There were few rooms in these constructions. The keepers had wood-paneled bedrooms, a storeroom, a kitchen with a tiny stove, and the watch room (also known as the service room). A spiral staircase wound up the inside of the tower to the external gallery from which the keeper surveyed the ocean. Rock lighthouses often have particularly wide bases to offer greater resistance to the huge waves that pummel them.

Scanning the sea for shipping accidents was one of the keepers' most important duties.

Buoy Layers

Nowadays, buoys are kept in place by long metal chains attached to a concrete weight on the seabed.

The coast guard and other world lighthouse authorities use many kinds of boats to perform their tasks. One of these is the buoy layer, which is used for laying and maintaining luminous buoys at sea. They were, until recently, very long, slender ships with pointed bows, impressive fore-and-aft bridges, and a flat deck for storing the buoys and their long chains. Another distinctive feature was the crane mounted toward the prow, which lifted the enormous buoy before dropping it into the sea.

Nowadays, smaller, lighter plastic buoys have replaced the cavernous metal balls of the past. And there is no need to keep stocks of gas on board because the lamps draw power from solar panels. So buoy layers have adapted and are now much lighter, more squat ships. The crew normally consists of a dozen sailors who set off every week to inspect several hundred miles of coastline.

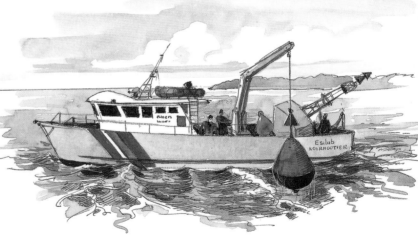

The new buoy layers are smaller and more maneuverable.

Lightships

The lightship *Channel,* stationed in the English Channel, is one of the last to brave the swell night and day. There are only some twenty or so lightships left in the world.

In places where no rock lighthouse could be built—for example, on sand banks where the soil was unstable, or in places where construction work was impossible even at low tide—lightships used to be necessary. They were held in place by two long chains with heavy anchors. In the middle of the ship was a tall metal tower carrying the lantern. At first, lightships were not motorized and had to be towed into position. When a storm came, they simply rode the waves. The keepers were often seasick as the boat pitched up and down like a cork. Sometimes fierce storms pulled an anchor loose and set the lightship adrift. It was vital to find the lightship and tow it back, but that could take hours—before the invention of radio there was no way to know where it had gone! Lightships were mostly replaced in the 1980s by very large automatic buoys, but until then ships entering many North Sea ports always encountered these strange-looking vessels.

The lightship *Le Havre* is now in a museum in the city of Le Havre, France—the city after which it was named.

Which Lighthouse Was That?

▲ Lighthouses on the Seine River (France)

▼ Longships Lighthouse (England)

Colored beams of light flash over the sea by night. As darkness falls, the dance of the lighthouses begins.

▲ La Courbe Lighthouse (France)

Lighthouses do not only alert ships to the presence of the coast, they also help them figure out where they are. If they were all exactly the same—if they all had the same color of light and a fixed beam like a star—they would be no help with orientation. In the nineteenth century, ships' captains sometimes mistook one lighthouse for another. So it was decided that the beam of each one should be different. Now every lighthouse has its own identifiable code, which sailors must be able to recognize. It is a bit like Morse code: The navigator must count the number and duration of the flashes, then look them up in a book called the *Lights List* or check on a map. This tells him which lighthouse signal he's seeing and where that lighthouse is. Some lighthouses have flashing lights, some have revolving beams, others are fixed and constant. There are even lighthouses with red beams to distinguish them from other nearby lights.

The revolving beam of a lighthouse—a reassuring sight for navigators.

How Were Lighthouses Built?

All rock lighthouses are immensely solid to protect them against the impact of waves. They are made of concrete, or of stone like Bishop Rock, left. The first Bishop Rock Lighthouse was swept away but was almost entirely reconstructed. Metallic towers are too fragile for such locations.

Building a lighthouse often called for great engineering skill since they were usually located in very exposed and inaccessible places. In the nineteenth century, the engineers were assisted by stonecutters and masons. The construction of the lighthouse tower—square, pyramidal, conical, or octagonal—would begin with the piling up of thousands of blocks of stones. Each of these would be joined on its top, side, and bottom to the stones around it to ensure the solidity of the whole. Construction often took a very long time. A coastal lighthouse might take two years to build, but the Bishop Rock Lighthouse (completed in 1858 on a reef off the Scilly Islands in southwestern England) took seven years, and the Ar-Men Lighthouse in France took fourteen years, from 1867 to 1881. The Ar-Men Lighthouse engineers had to contend with severe storms that might demolish the half-constructed building. In less exposed sites, lighthouse builders used less sturdy materials. There is a wooden lighthouse on Prince Edward Island in Canada and a metal one on Foerder Island in Norway. Buildings like this could be made of small components that could be carried by hand up the steep paths and then assembled on the site.

In the nineteenth century, building a lighthouse was a huge enterprise that might last several years.

The Stairs

The staircase of a lighthouse spirals upward like a snail in its shell. The space in the center of the stairwell is used to haul equipment up with a rope.

A lighthouse keeper had to be physically fit. The staircase was long and steep. It has been calculated that a keeper in a tall tower climbed around two million steps over the course of a forty-year career—since each step was about eight inches high, he would have traveled about 250 miles. The staircase is "rolled up" in the center of the tower like a snail in its shell, the brass handrail shining in the light of the small lighthouse windows. There are stories of obsessively clean keepers who refused to touch the handrail for fear of spoiling its shine. Internal walls were sometimes covered with tiles made of opaline (a kind of glass that is a bit like bathroom tiles) so that they were not affected by condensation. This was important because the staircase might otherwise become slippery and dangerous. One keeper at least is known to have died after falling down the stairs in his lighthouse. Some lighthouses, when they were reconstructed after World War II, had elevators installed. What luxury!

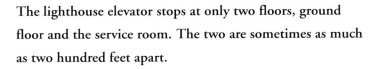

The lighthouse elevator stops at only two floors, ground floor and the service room. The two are sometimes as much as two hundred feet apart.

The Lantern

Some lanterns feature sculptures ornamented with stars, lion-headed gutters, and weathervanes showing the wind direction.

All lighthouses wear the strange "glass cap" which protects the lantern but allows light in and out. The earliest lanterns were made of stone and had tiny windows with bars; little light came in and not much went out! Around 1770 the lantern first began to adopt its present form: a six-, eight-, or ten-sided metal crown with a copper dome. It was set on a little circular supporting wall and surrounded by the gallery. A lightning conductor was another vital addition. Diligent care was taken with the lantern: The glass had to be cleaned regularly and any panes broken by wind or stormy seas had to be replaced at once. The keepers sometimes had to climb out onto the dome, too—some 200 feet up from the ground!—to repair the weathervane or check the state of the gutters. The gutters were used to collect rainwater, which then poured out of little lion-headed sculptures that resembled the gargoyles on cathedrals. From there it ran into a cistern and was used for drinking water.

In small stone lanterns, soot from the fire soon clouded the panes.

The Earth Is Round!

The small Barra Head Lighthouse in Scotland is higher than the taller Île de Vierge Lighthouse in France, since it rests on cliffs more than six hundred feet above sea level.

The beam of a lighthouse is projected from the top of a high tower or from buildings on cliffs or hills. Why is this? The answer is very simple: Because the earth is round. When you look at the ocean, you see no farther than the horizon, the line that divides sea and sky. If you want to see beyond this point, you must gain height. Stand on tiptoe and you can see a little bit farther. If you climb up a tower, you are much higher again and can see farther still. For a child looking out to sea from a beach, the horizon is about two nautical miles away. Climbing a hundred-foot tower increases this distance to eleven nautical miles. A little more climbing takes you up a hill 500 feet above sea level; now you can see a ship twenty-five nautical miles away. Walk back down to the beach and it will have vanished! Lighthouses exemplify this principle. They are built so tall because they must be visible from very far away.

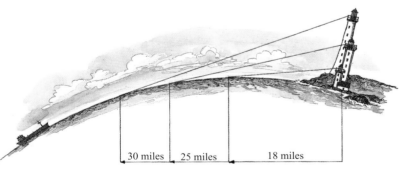

30 miles   25 miles   18 miles

The height of a building determines the distance it can be seen from.

The Fresnel Lens

A Fresnel optic is made of hundreds of glass components held in a brass frame. Cleaning them means hours of work.

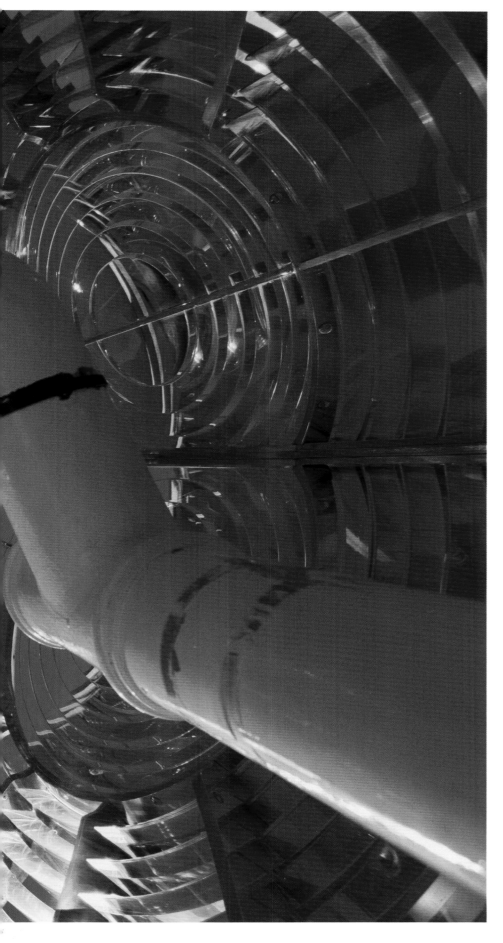

In 1825, Augustin Fresnel invented something very important for every lighthouse in the world: the Fresnel lens. This lens causes all the rays from a light source to shine in one direction, focusing the beam of light. Lenses and prisms can be used to change the direction of a ray of light (this is called refraction). Fresnel arranged concentric rings of glass prisms around a central lens so that all the light was collected into a single intense beam. By setting the rings of glass at the correct angle on a flat surface, he was able to make his lens enormously powerful. To make a flashing light, for example, he would place four of his lenses upright around the outside of a circle and rotate them. These lenses can be enormous—some of them are over six feet wide and ten feet high. And the effect is extraordinary, as if the eye of a giant Cyclops were illuminating the horizon!

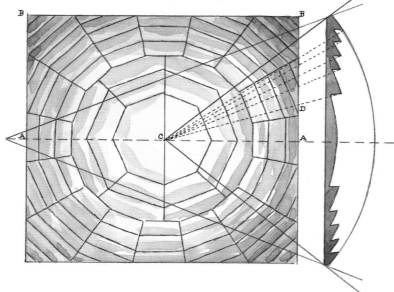

A Fresnel lens, like the projector in a movie theater, focuses all the available light in a single direction.

The Mercury Trough

A lighthouse beam turns in the dark. The Carteret Lighthouse in France lies on a very dangerous cross-channel shortcut, the Déroute Passage.

Lighthouses are recognized by the character of their light beams. Some have a fixed beam, others a rotating beam. To make the beam of light go around, the whole Fresnel lens assembly (called the optic) has to be rotated—and it can be as heavy as an elephant! The solution to this problem is very ingenious: Imagine a big rubber innertube floating in a swimming pool. Not only will it hold your weight, but you can easily make it spin around. This is because it moves so smoothly over the water. The same technique was used in lighthouses. The lens assembly was placed on a ring floating on a vat of liquid metal (mercury) so that it could turn almost without friction. The vat is called a mercury trough. Using this, the lighthouse keeper could turn the entire apparatus, weighing several tons, with his little finger! The rotation could therefore continue almost indefinitely and was powered by clockwork (which the keepers had to remember to wind up). Imagine being able to spin an elephant around with your little finger . . .

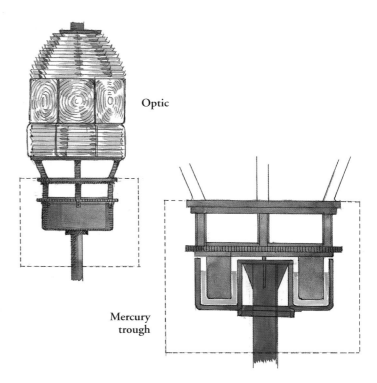

Optic

Mercury trough

The ring (shown in brown) floats on the mercury (shown in blue) like a rubber innertube on water.

The Lighthouse Keeper

The keeper of Silleiro Lighthouse in northern Spain checks the bulbs. If one fails, it is automatically replaced.

The automation of lighthouses was completed about ten years ago, but until then every lighthouse had at least one and sometimes several keepers. They wore Coast Guard uniforms and it was their job to make sure that the lantern was always working properly. The signal must never, never, never be allowed to go out at night. This was a heavy responsibility: One mistake might result in a shipwreck. In the early twentieth century, for each thirty days keepers spent on the job they had ten days off. But if they were working on a rock lighthouse, they could never be sure how long they would be on duty. Storms might stop the crew on its way to replace them. In that case, the keepers simply had to stay put. In 1929, two keepers of the Veille Lighthouse in France remained prisoners of the weather for forty-five days past their regular tour of duty. Fortunately they had sufficient food reserves to survive.

The keeper's uniform was his pride and joy when welcoming visitors to the lighthouse.

Relieving a Rock Lighthouse Keeper

Making a landing is sometimes dangerous. In this case the breeches buoy, rope, and pulley are used.

It was no easy matter to get a relief keeper from a boat to a rock lighthouse—or, for that matter, getting one from the lighthouse back to the boat. When the boat arrived, a double rope with a pulley was thrown down from the light-house gallery and secured. A breeches buoy (a ring-shaped life buoy with support in the form of short "breeches," or pant legs) was attached to it. The relief keeper got into the breeches buoy and was then drawn up to the gallery. It sounds simple, but you must remember that the boat was bobbing up and down in the water and the waves could be high. For the most part, the keeper was suspended high above the waves, but sometimes he was caught by one. Imagine being the outgoing keeper, who had to watch all this before getting into the bouy himself, knowing exactly how severe a splashing he could expect.

Accidents like this could drown the keeper, but were very rare.

The Keepers' Accommodations

Sleeping arrangements at the Eddystone Lighthouse in England. Each keeper had his own cupboard, bed linen, and bed—a private corner often decorated with photos of his family.

When the lighthouse was located on the mainland or an island, the keeper and his family lived beside the tower. They generally had a kitchen, one or two bedrooms, an office, and a storeroom for lighting equipment. The furniture was there when they arrived: a big bed, a table, chairs, and a few kitchen utensils. But not much! Over the years, keepers' housing expanded and became more comfortable. Eventually they had something like a real home, complete with television sets and radios.

On rock lighthouses, things were very different. First of all, only the keeper lived there, separated from his family, who stayed on the mainland. For the keeper, winter was the harshest season. He had to put up with cold, humidity, and wind. Often the lighthouse was unheated. In French lighthouses, the best way of keeping warm was to snuggle down in the cupboard bed, which had doors that could be closed to keep in the warmth. Who would want to leave a bed like that for the midnight shift?

Cupboard beds were used mainly in French lighthouses.

Keeping the Light

"Housekeeping" was a requirement for lighthouse keepers. Neglect was punishable. A keeper at Chipiona Lighthouse in Spain is seen here cleaning the lantern panes.

The work of the keeper was hard and very repetitive. In addition to maintaining the optic, he had to keep the building shipshape, which meant constant cleaning. The windows had to be cleaned and the brass banister polished until it shone. No trace of dust was allowed in the service room with the lantern. The hundreds of rings of glass in the optic were meticulously polished every month. The clockwork mechanism that turned the optic had to be taken apart and checked periodically. The staircase, with as many as 260 steps, had to be swept clean. And the fuel (at first coal, later oils of various kinds) had to be hauled up to the lantern, before the days of electricity.

The work was divided between two keepers. Each had his own areas of expertise. One of them might prefer to take care of the brass frames around the lantern and the other of the optic itself. Some keepers worked with the same colleague in this way for more than twenty years. Keepers on the same tour of duty had to find each other's company agreeable because it was the only company they had.

Spit and polish was the rule and the brass handrail was kept immaculate.

51

Cooking and Keeping Busy

Fishing was an excellent way of improving meals, otherwise made up of canned food, dried fish, and hard biscuits.

Every keeper had his own way of keeping boredom at bay. Some made ships in bottles, sculpted ivory figurines, or repaired clocks and watches. Others preferred doing crossword puzzles. There was always a small library in the lighthouse. Some keepers took up painting. But most of them read the newspaper and waited for news of their families through the lighthouse's radio. Among their favorite occupations was cooking. If they were on a rock lighthouse, they would cast a fishing line and leave it, coming back at low tide to gather their catch. Some of these rock lighthouses even had fish pools built in, to keep the fish fresh. Many lighthouses throughout the world have their own recipes.

Keepers were masters at fishing from the base of their lighthouses.

Storms

If you were a keeper, which lighthouse would you choose to work in? The Le Four Lighthouse in France's Iroise Sea, below left; the Isle of Pilier Lighthouse, also in France, top left; or the St. Agnes Lighthouse (now a private home) in the Scilly Isles in England, right?

Lighthouse keepers did not mince their words. For French lighthouse men, each lighthouse was either a "hell," "purgatory," or "paradise." English lighthouse keepers were less theological but had strong opinions all the same. Keepers' least favorite types of towers to work in were rock lighthouses, and English keepers had a particular fear of the lighthouse on Wolf Rock off Land's End, where waves sometimes washed clear over the 134-foot tower. On Fastnet, on the southern tip of Ireland, the keepers lived in fear of the tower coming down in a storm. There they were imprisoned by the sea, sometimes surviving on stale bread because the seas were too stormy for the supply boat to get through.

Life was a little less harsh on the island lighthouses. These towers had a little more space: One could sometimes stretch one's legs on the islet if the swell was low, but storms might still inundate the keeper's cottage or prevent the supply boats from reaching the island.

And there were one or two lighthouse "paradises," such as the Île de Batz Lighthouse in France, or Alfanzina in Portugal. Imagine a pretty little cottage down by the sea, with a little vegetable plot and chickens clucking around the house—perhaps even a cow for fresh milk. What more could you want?

Only after some thirty years of arduous service could a keeper expect a cushy position like this.

The Keeper by Night

The light must never go out—its revolving beam keeps watch at sea. Hundreds of thousands of ships have reason to be grateful to the Creac'h Lighthouse on the island of Ushant in France.

In every lighthouse, the lamp was lit just before sunset. This was done following a calendar which specified—to the minute—when the light should go on. The keeper went up to the lantern a good half hour earlier to prepare the lamp and recheck the equipment. Once the flame was steady (before electricity) and the optic revolving—literally "like clockwork"—he would retire to a service room on the story beneath, where he spent his duty hours. Exactly in the middle of the night, he was replaced by his colleague, who worked until dawn, then cleaned the optic and prepared things for the following night. As a result, the two keepers might only meet once or twice a day. How strange a job it must have seemed to some of these keepers—stuck in the tower for weeks at a time, repeating the same tasks day after day. They often found the solitude unbearable.

A keeper on duty in the service room.

Automation

A technological miracle, automated lighthouses ensure faultless service by making provisions for any conceivable technical failure.

Automation marked the end of the harsh and lonely life of the lighthouse keeper. Attempts had been made since 1880 to replace the crews with some kind of automatic mechanism. This, it was thought, would solve everything, but it turned out not to be so. It was not just a question of turning the light on and off—mechanical failure had to be completely ruled out. How could this be done without anyone to check the equipment? Full automation finally became possible some twenty years ago with the advent of halogen bulbs. Nowadays, when these fail, a small mechanism substitutes a new one. If the solar panels fail, batteries or gas engines kick in. If an accident occurs, a radio message is automatically sent out requesting repairs. So everything is taken care of, right? Well, not completely. For one thing, the now empty lighthouses are falling into disrepair because no one is looking after them. Automation was an economic necessity, but as a result, many lighthouses themselves are in physical decline.

This modern lighthouse has a wind turbine and solar panels for electricity generation, a small optic, and a very compact and economical lamp.

The Sailors' Guardian

Keeping watch at the Sein Lighthouse in France. Direct observation of meteorological conditions and military and civil traffic was part of the keeper's job.

Lighthouses helped every vessel, whatever its nationality, size, or power, to find its way through the night, thus ensuring the safety of yacht and oil tanker alike. This service has been provided for more than three hundred years around the world. And it costs the sailor nothing. Throughout the world, lighthouses project their kindly beams over the ocean waves.

Lighthouse keepers were often the first witnesses of a shipwreck, and informed the ports and coast guards. They would often rescue the stranded sailors themselves, giving them shelter, food, and drink in the lighthouse. In this way, keepers saved many lives and their very presence was reassuring. The ocean was not such a lonely place. Since automation, the lighthouses stand empty and there are no friendly eyes scanning the waves for danger.

Rescues like this were rare, but the keepers' presence was reassuring.

Helicopters

Two methods are used for getting men onto a lighthouse by helicopter. Equipment and men can be landed on a helipad on the top of the tower, left, or the technician can be lowered onto the gallery, right.

▼ Kéréon Lighthouse (France)

Rock lighthouses are now completely automatic and their doors are locked. You cannot reach the optic by striding up the stairs or climbing a ladder. The boats that supplied the lighthouses have been replaced by helicopters. Coast Guard officials say it's much cheaper this way. And it is true that supply boats often failed to land supplies when the waves were too high. Since a helicopter is not at the mercy of storm and tide, the lighthouse is accessible at any time. The technicians who have replaced the keepers now enter the tower from the top, hung from the helicopter like fish on a line and gently let down onto the gallery, although many lighthouses now have their own helipad on top of the lantern. At first, this must have been quite an experience: the motor roaring, the pilot shouting "Go!" when you have to jump out, then the violent turbulence from the rotor blades making you swing on the end of your rope. What a relief to set foot on the lighthouse! But the technicians soon grew used to all that.

Repairs

Building work on a lighthouse is always a major undertaking. At left, the dome of Porquerolles Lighthouse in France is renovated. On the right, Banche Lighthouse, also in France, is repainted. Maintenance of these buildings requires thousands of hours.

Lighthouses are generally located in exposed places. However, seawater erodes masonry, sand abrades paint, water seeps into the lantern, buoys are carried away by the current, and wind flattens the weathervane. So after every storm, checks must be made. Has the beacon been blown over? Have all the lantern's panes survived intact? The process of monitoring is now automated and problems are immediately reported by radio. Buoys set adrift are quickly located and recovered. Control centers act immediately to make repairs, many of which are performed by former keepers who now work from the mainland. Such repairs are vital to the safety of shipping. But it should be remembered that today only one percent of the light signals managed by organizations such as the U.S. Coast Guard are lighthouses. Most maritime signals are smaller lights serving yachters and those who sail for pleasure. Lighthouses are now lost among this myriad of smaller lights.

Equipment for lighthouse maintenance is loaded onto a boat.

Satellite-Aided Navigation

Leaving Portsmouth harbor in England, the captain of a Brittany Ferry scans his radar screens to orient himself in the fairway. In places with high volumes of traffic, the use of electronic aids is imperative.

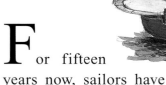

For fifteen years now, sailors have had access to a new positioning system more effective than the visual clues afforded by lighthouses. This is called GPS (Global Positioning System) or DGPS (Differential Global Positioning System). A little computer aboard a boat uses a network of satellites to fix its position within a couple of yards. And it can do this at any time and in any weather. You might think that this would render the lanterns and other signal lights obsolete, but in fact the lesser lights—harbor and range lights and the luminous buoys marking dangers or navigable channels—are still much appreciated and widely used. It is the great lighthouses themselves that are being ignored. They do, however, offer a backup for ships whose GPS has broken down; and sailors want them maintained for that purpose. But the most handsome lighthouses are already being promoted as tourist or heritage attractions.

A satellite

Color Sectors

The Cordouan Lighthouse signposts the mouth of the Gironde River in France, alerting sailors to the sandbanks on either side of the fairway.

Lighthouses "speak" to sailors. A language and a vocabulary have been invented so that they can make themselves clear. Colored lights form part of this language. The principle of a white, or safe, zone surrounded by different color sectors was established throughout the world in 1977. "Sector lights" flash different colors in different directions. Whenever the navigator sees red or green, danger is imminent. If you are following a beam of white light into the harbor and suddenly the beam turns red, take evasive action—you are entering shallow water. Look for the white beam again to guide you to safety. The same colors are found on buoys marking navigable channels. Stay with the white, keep away from the colors!

However, to follow this advice you have to know where in the world you are. In Europe, Australia, Africa, and the Gulf countries, the port (left) marker is red and the starboard (right) marker is green. In America and Asia, the opposite is true. So make sure you know where you are before you lose your way!

The simple colored plates enable the beam of light to take on different hues.

Steering for Port

Two towers, two colors, one ship that sails in the night: a harbor like most harbors in the world.

Ships entering or leaving a port must follow the fairway, a sort of traffic corridor, which is narrow and relatively shallow. The object is to keep to the center of this channel. To help the navigator, a system of alignment is used. One light, generally at sea or at the end of a jetty, is lined up with a second, which is generally on land and higher up than the first. The captain has only to make sure that the two lights stay one right above the other to be sure of his direction. The slightest divergence is immediately visible. To create signals like these, two towers had to be constructed several miles apart at different heights.

Having successfully negotiated the channel, the captain encounters the red and green beacons that frame the entrances to ports worldwide. "Welcome home!" they seem to say.